For the daydreamers, you're perfect as you are.

AF426610

A NOTE ABOUT THIS BOOK:

My ADHD Monster is a children's book written to help kids who are struggling with an ADHD diagnosis. This book is NOT a diagnostic tool and no book can replace therapy or medical opinion.

If you are seeking information on next steps for your child, you can visit my website at chivaunoldes.com and check out the resources tab for links to help.

This is my monster.
She lives in my
brain and makes
it work differently.

She makes it hard for me to pay attention in school.

Sometimes she makes
me daydream when I
should be listening.

DO HOMEWORK TONIGHT

She makes it hard for
me to stay
organized.
8

Sometimes I am clumsy or forgetful.

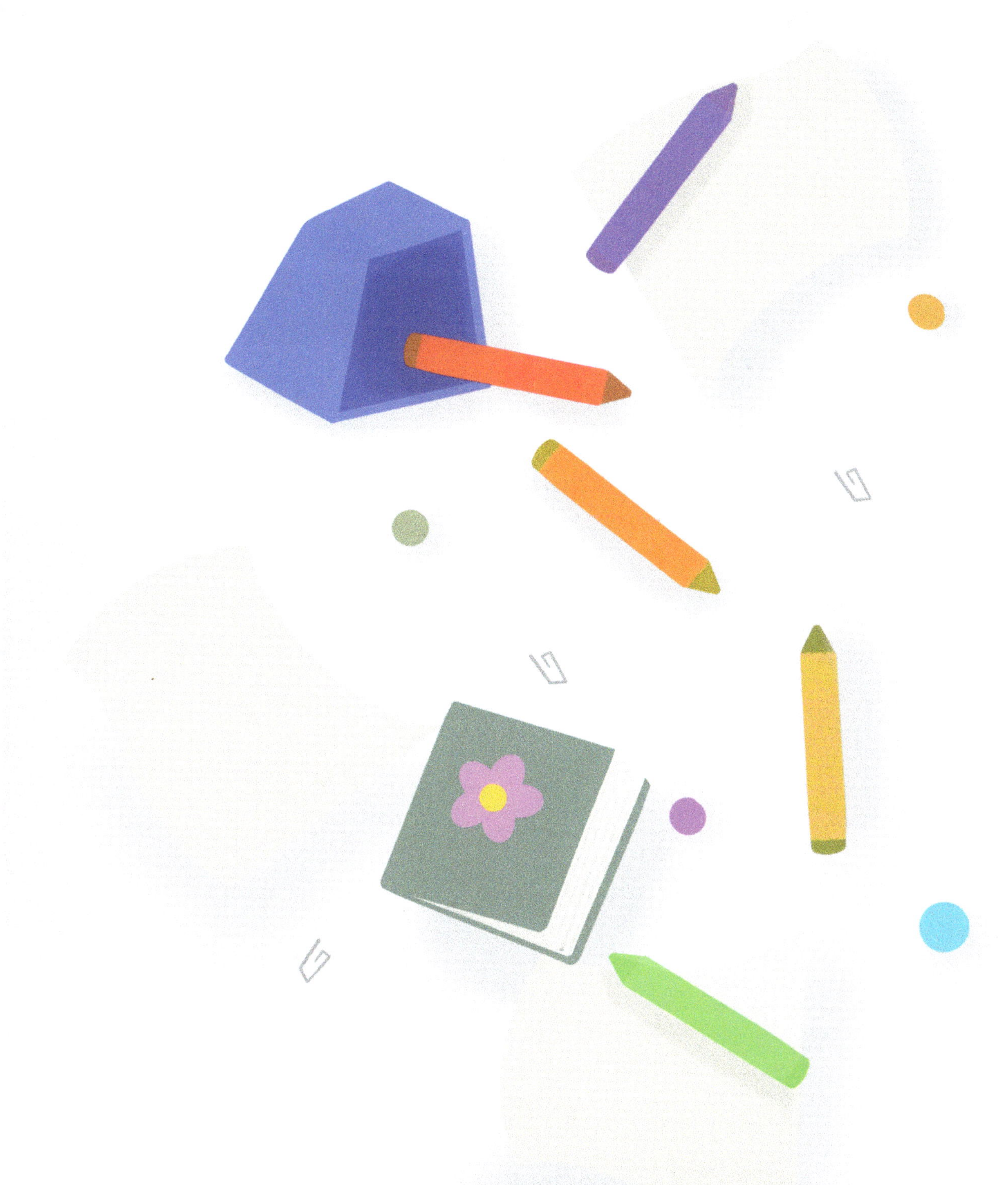

Name: Sarah

1. Draw a square.

2. Draw a circle.

Sometimes I make silly mistakes, even when I know better, because I'm going too fast or not paying attention.

I talk to the grown-ups in my life and together we work to tame my monster and keep her calm.

I talk to a therapist. She is like a doctor for my brain. We name my monster ADHD. That stands for Inattentive Attention Deficit Hyperactivity Disorder.

Rx

We work together to make a plan for taming my monster. We also decide if I should take medicine to help her stay quiet during school.

Having a routine for each day can help me to keep on task. Checklists, sticker charts, and behavior trackers are helpful.

MORNING ROUTINE
Eat breakfast
Get dressed
Brush teeth
Do hair
Put on shoes
20

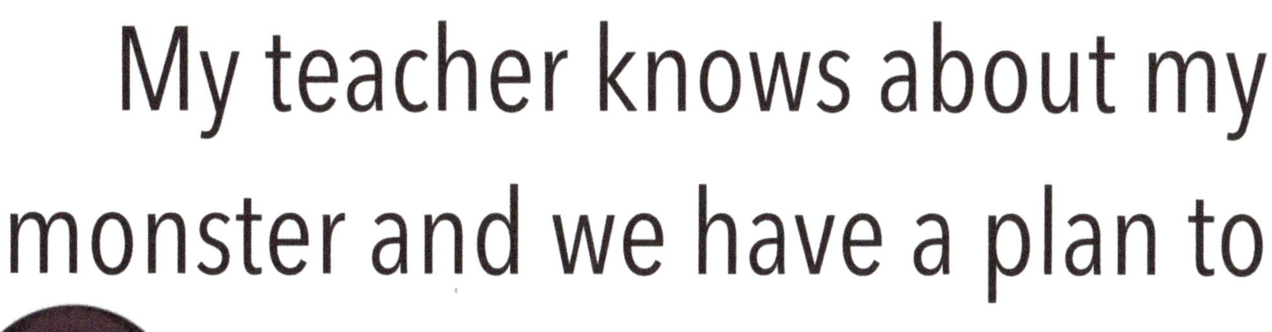

My teacher knows about my monster and we have a plan to help me do well in school.

Blah, blah,
blah, blah...

When I am working on something that I need to focus on, it's important that I don't have distractions like music, TV, or loud noises.

My parents make sure to give me simple, easy-to-follow directions when they ask me to do something.

Sometimes I feel very mad at my monster because she makes my brain different from my friends.

But my monster also makes me feel special. She helps me to imagine, create, and dream up things that nobody else can.

My monster is a part of me and she always will be. I guess that makes her pretty special too.

www.ingramcontent.com/pod-product-compliance
Lightning Source LLC
Chambersburg PA
CBHW041823110726
48006CB00019B/2483